The Jurassic Dinosaurs

The editors gratefully thank Claudia Berghaus, Diane Gabriel, and the Geology Section of the Milwaukee Public Museum for their enthusiastic cooperation and technical assistance. And thanks, too, to Matthew Peterson, second grader at Catholic East Elementary School in Milwaukee, for his invaluable assistance.

Library of Congress Cataloging-in-Publication Data

Burton, Jane.
    The Jurassic Dinosaurs.

    (The New dinosaur library)
    Includes index.
    Summary: Brief text and illustrations introduce the characteristics and natural environment of eleven dinosaurs of the Jurassic period including Diplodocus, Stegosaurus, and Cryptocleidus. Also contains a glossary and miscellaneous facts about dinosaurs.
    1. Dinosaurs--Juvenile literature. 2. Paleontology--Juvenile literature. 2. Paleontology--Jurassic--Juvenile literature. [1. Dinosaurs. 2. Paleontology--Jurassic] I. Kirk, Steve, ill. II. Dixon, Dougal. III. Title. IV. Series.
QE862.D5B85   1987   567.9'1   87-6462
ISBN 1-55532-285-9
ISBN 1-55532-260-3 (lib. bdg.)

This North American edition first published in 1987 by

Gareth Stevens, Inc.
7317 West Green Tree Road Milwaukee, WI 53223, USA

This US edition copyright © 1987. Based on *The Age of Dinosaurs*, by Jane Burton and Dougal Dixon, conceived and produced by Eddison/Sadd Editions, London, and first published in the United Kingdom and Australia by Sphere Books, London, 1984, and in the United States of America, under the title *Time Exposure*, by Beaufort Books, New York, 1984.

Design: Laurie Shock.
Background photography in selected photos: Norman Tomalin, Paul Wakefield, David Houston.
Photo retouching: Kay Robinson, with the exception of pages 6-7 by Brian Bull.
Line drawings: Laurie Shock and Paul Robinson.
Additional text: MaryLee Knowlton.
Series editors: MaryLee Knowlton & Mark Sachner.

Technical consultant: Diane Gabriel, Assistant Curator of Paleontology, Milwaukee Public Museum.

4 5 6 7 8 9 92 91 90 89 88

The Jurassic Dinosaurs

Photography by
Jane Burton

Text by
Dougal Dixon

Artwork of Photographed Reptiles by
Steve Kirk

Gareth Stevens Publishing
Milwaukee

THE NEW DINOSAUR LIBRARY

Hunting
the
Dinosaurs
and Other Prehistoric Animals

The
First
Dinosaurs

The
Jurassic
Dinosaurs

The
Last
Dinosaurs

The Jurassic Dinosaurs

The first reptiles appeared 345 million years ago and gave rise to the dinosaurs. The Age of Dinosaurs is made up of three periods — the Triassic, the Jurassic, and the Cretaceous. This book is about dinosaurs and other prehistoric animals of the *Jurassic* period. The Jurassic period came between the Triassic and Cretaceous periods. It lasted for 55 million years, ending 135 million years ago.

During this time, the world was still just one land mass. Dinosaurs roamed freely from what would be Africa today to South America. The Earth was warming up, and plants grew where none had grown before. Both meat-eating and plant-eating dinosaurs had plenty of food. The reign of the dinosaurs continued.

CONTENTS

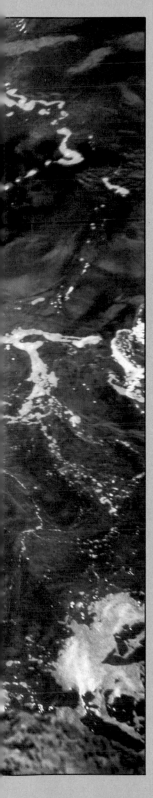

CRYPTOCLEIDUS

Cryptocleidus was a swimming reptile. It had a turtle-shaped body and paddle-like limbs. Its long snaky neck stretched high above the water. Because of its neck, Cryptocleidus was nicely *adapted* for catching fish.

One of Cryptocleidus' cousins was Elasmosaurus. This animal grew to lengths of 32 ft (10 m)!

CRYPTOCLEIDUS (crip-toe-KLI-dus)

Length: 10 ft (3 m)   Location: England

Order: Sauropterygia

Cryptocleidus' neck was very flexible, and its jaws had many sharp, pointed teeth. It was well-suited for catching fish.

7

METRIORHYNCHUS

Metriorhynchus was an early type of crocodile. It was different from crocodiles of today. It too was *descended* from a land animal, but it developed completely into a sea-living animal.

Its legs became swimming paddles. The body became smooth and streamlined. Its tail had a fin at the end. It looked similar to a fish.

Today's crocodile is older than Metriorhynchus. Metriorhynchus was completely adapted to its marine *environment*.

METRIORHYNCHUS (MEH-tree-o-RIN-cus)

Length: 10 ft (3 m)   Order: Crocodilia
Location: Europe and South America

The crocodile (2) still looks like its Triassic ancestors who lived both in water and on land. Metriorhynchus (1) looks more like a fish.

OPHTHALMOSAURUS

Ophthalmosaurus was perfectly adapted to life in the sea. Like today's shark and dolphin, it had a large fin on its back. This probably helped it keep its balance.

Ophthalmosaurus was *piscivorous*, or a fish-eater, but it had no teeth. Its large eyes probably helped it see well and catch slower-moving fish even in dimly lit water.

Fossils have shown Ophthalmosaurus giving birth to live babies. Its dolphin-like body kept it from leaving the water to lay eggs.

OPHTHALMOSAURUS (off-THAL-mo-saw-rus)
Length: 10 ft (3 m)   Location: England
Subclass: Ichthyopterygia

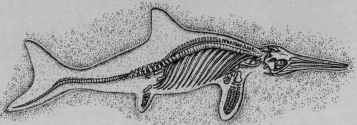

Sometimes the *impression* of an ichthyosaur like
Ophthalmosaurus is preserved in the rock that surrounds
its skeleton. Ichthyosaurs were sea animals.

COMPSOGNATHUS

Compsognathus was the size of a chicken. It was one of the smallest of the *carnivorous*, or meat-eating, dinosaurs.

Compsognathus had three toes on its legs but only two fingers on its hands. In this way, the smallest meat-eater resembled the largest —Tyrannosaurus.

COMPSOGNATHUS (comp-sog-NATH-us)

Length: 2 ft (60 cm)   Order: Saurischia

Location: Bavaria and southeast France

This skeleton was found with its
head twisted back and its tail pulled
up. This happened as the tendons
of the spine dried and shrank after
the Compsognathus died.

A few specimens of Archaeopteryx have been found. They show a dinosaur-like skeleton with feathers and hollow bones.

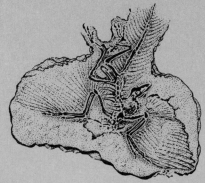

ARCHAEOPTERYX

Paleontologists call Archaeopteryx the first bird. Its skeleton was like Compsognathus, which was a dinosaur. But it was covered with feathers like today's birds. Feathers are just *modified* scales. They probably developed as *insulation* to keep Archaeopteryx warm. Unlike modern birds, Archaeopteryx had teeth, claws on its wings, and a long, bony tail.

Archaeopteryx probably glided from trees to the ground. It had weak wing muscles, so it probably climbed back up the trees using its clawed wings and feet.

ARCHAEOPTERYX (ar-kee-OP-ter-ix)	
Length: 1 ft (30 cm)	Weight: 18 oz (500 gm)
Location: southern Germany	Order: Aves

PTERODACTYLUS

Pterodactylus was about the size of a pigeon. It had much larger wings, though. Also, Pterodactylus did not have feathers. Its wings were formed by a leathery *membrane*. This membrane stretched from the body to the *elongated* fourth fingers and to the legs.

Like birds, Pterodactylus had light, hollow bones. Its body was covered with fur. This could mean that Pterodactylus may have been able to control its body heat, like today's mammals and birds.

PTERODACTYLUS (ter-o-DAC-teh-lus)

Length: 9 in (22 cm)   Wingspan: 10 in (25 cm)
Location: southern Germany   Order: Pterosauria

We can tell the diet of animals by looking at their teeth. Pterodaustro (1) scooped plankton from the water; Anurognathus (2) ate insects; Dorygnathus (3) ate meat; and Pteranodon (4) caught fish.

No Apatosaurus skull was found till *1979*! Scientists were surprised that it was so long and slender, like that of Diplodocus. They had thought it would be square.

APATOSAURUS

Between the Rocky Mountains and the shallow inland sea were flood plains 150 million years ago. Here Apatosaurus lived, feeding on the needles of *conifers* that grew in green forests on these plains. Paleontologists have found many tracks that suggest Apatosaurus traveled in herds sheltering its young in the center.

Many people know Apatosaurus as Brontosaurus. Apatosaurus means "headless lizard." Early remains were found without heads.

APATOSAURUS (uh-PAT-o-saw-rus)

Length: 65 ft (20 m)   Weight: 30 tons
Location: Colorado   Order: Saurischia

DIPLODOCUS

Diplodocus was very long. But it was a light-weight compared to similar dinosaurs. It probably lived in herds that moved from one feeding spot to another.

Diplodocus probably ate mostly conifer needles and other tough plants. But the few peg-like teeth in the front of its jaw would not have been very good for chewing. Diplodocus probably swallowed stones to help grind up food inside its *gizzard* — just like the birds of today.

DIPLODOCUS (dip-LOD-uh-cus)

Length: 91 ft (28 m)

Order: Saurischia   Location: Utah

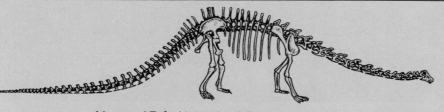

About 45 ft (14 m) of Diplodocus' 91 ft (28 m) was tail, and 30 ft (8 m) was neck.

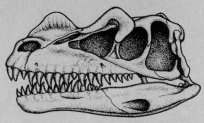

Ceratosaurus had a skull that was formed by light, loosely hinged bones. The jaws stretched so it could gulp down large chunks of meat.

CERATOSAURUS

Ceratosaurus was a medium-sized but powerful carnivorous dinosaur. Its shorter front legs had four-clawed fingers, and its back legs had three-clawed toes. Ceratosaurus used its huge hind claws and smaller front claws as killing weapons. Fossils tracks show that Ceratosaurus may have hunted in packs, like wolves.

Ceratosaurus had a horn on its nose and a heavy ridge over its eyes. These may have been used to attract female ceratosaurs or to scare away enemies.

CERATOSAURUS (seh-RAT-o-saw-rus)

Length: 19 ft (6 m)   Order: Saurischia
Location: Colorado, Wyoming, and East Africa

COELURUS

Coelurus ate animals that it hunted. It also was a *scavenger*, eating rotting *carcasses* of animals killed by larger dinosaurs.

On its front limbs, Coelurus had three fingers. One faced the other two. The single finger was used as a thumb to hold things.

Coelurus was shaped like the large meat-eating dinosaurs. It was much lighter, however. It moved more quickly and could probably jump to catch flying animals.

COELURUS (seh-LURE-us)

Length: 6 ft (2 m)   Weight: 66 lb (30 kg)

Location: Wyoming   Order: Saurischia

The skeleton of
Coelurus was like that
of the other large meat-
eaters, but it was more
lightly built. Its skull
was about the size of a
human hand.

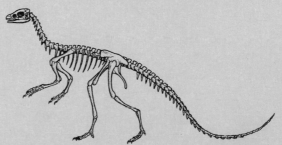

Three ways the plates along the back of Stegosaurus could have been arranged.

STEGOSAURUS

Stegosaurus had a double row of plates along its back. No one knows for sure why they were there or how they were arranged. Perhaps they protected Stegosaurus from meat-eaters. They also may have absorbed warmth from the sun to warm the body or given off heat to cool the body. Where the plates stop Stegosaurus had a double row of spikes. It may have used its strong tail and fearsome spikes to protect itself from *predators*.

Stegosaurus was a plant-eater. It walked on all four legs. Its two-ton weight made it move quite slowly.

STEGOSAURUS (steg-o-SAW-rus)	
Length: 29 ft (9 m)	Height at hips: 8 ft (2-3 m)
Location: Colorado	Order: Ornithischia

Fun Facts About Dinosaurs

1. In August, 1966, 2,000 fossil dinosaur tracks were discovered in Rocky Hill, Connecticut. Fifteen hundred of them have been reburied for preservation. You can see the remaining 500, which are sheltered by a geodesic dome. The exact type of dinosaur has not yet been identified. It is probably from the early Jurassic period. It is thought to be related to Dilothosaurus, whose remains have been found in Arizona. The fossil site is now called Dinosaur State Park.

2. Here are some animals that appeared during the Age of Dinosaurs. They are still here today:

   turtles — late Triassic period
   crocodiles — late Triassic period
   sharks (pre-sharks) — Carboniferous period
   skates and rays — upper Cretaceous period

3. The feathers of Archaeopteryx were arranged like those of modern birds, with nine primary and fourteen secondary feathers. Primary feathers are the feathers that are actually inserted in the bones of the wing. They are the feathers that the animal actually uses for flying. Secondary feathers fill out the collection of feathers and make up the gliding part of the wing.

4. Ultrasaurus, the largest, tallest, and heaviest of all dinosaurs, lived in Jurassic times. Ultrasaurus was 100-115 ft (30-35 m) long, 56 ft (17 m) tall, and weighed in at 100-140 tons. The smallest dinosaur, Saltopus, lived during the late Triassic period. As an adult, it measured only 2 ft (60 cm) long.

5. Archaeopteryx had weak flight muscles. But it had strong claws. It probably clawed its way up a tree and glided back down.

6. Diplodocus and Brachiosaurus were two dinosaurs whose nostrils were above their eyes. Brachiosaurus may have had a trunk.

7. The animals that we call dinosaurs are actually two subgroups of the group called Archosauria. These two subgroups are Ornithischia, which means "bird-hipped," and Saurischia, which means "lizard-hipped." Both groups include some dinosaurs that walked on two feet and some that walked on four feet. Both groups also include meat-eaters and plant-eaters. The division of dinosaurs into Ornithischia or Saurischia is based on the types of pelvis or hips they have.

8. Both dinosaurs and pterosaurs, which were flying and gliding reptiles, belonged to the group Archosauria. The crocodile of today is also an archosaur.

9. Some dinosaurs had thick-walled bones to support their weight. Others had hollows in their spinal bones and holes in their skulls to reduce their weight. The lighter ones could probably move faster.

10. The Dinosaur National Museum in Jensen, Utah, is made up entirely of dinosaurs from the Jurassic period.

11. Here are the meanings of the names of some Jurassic dinosaurs:

> *Compsognathus* means "elegant jaw."
> *Archaeopteryx* means "primitive wing."
> *Pterodactylus* means "winged fingers."
> *Ceratosaurus* means "horned face."
> *Coelurus* means "hollow tail."
> *Stegosaurus* means "roof reptile."

12. Plant-eating dinosaurs had teeth that could grind their food, and some had a horny beak for nipping off plants. Some plant-eaters had several rows, or batteries, of teeth—often up to 2,000 in their mouth at one time. Also, unlike humans, who come with only two sets of teeth, all dinosaurs had continuous tooth replacement.

13. Meat-eating dinosaurs had very strong jaws and sharp teeth that could rip flesh from their prey. Usually meat-eaters were very strong and had vicious claws.

14. Scientists know that Compsognathus ate lizards because lizard bones have been found inside its rib cage.

More Books About Dinosaurs

Here are some more books about dinosaurs and other animals of their time. If you see any you would like to read, see if your library or bookstore has them.

The Age of Dinosaurs! Parker (Gareth Stevens)
All New Dinosaurs and Their Friends from the Great Recent Discoveries. Long & Welles (Bellerphon)
Archaeopteryx. Oliver (Rourke)
Digging Up Dinosaurs. Aliki (Harper & Row)
Dinosaurs and Their Young. Freedman (Holiday House)
Dinosaur Time. Parish (Starstream Products)
Diplodocus. Wilson (Rourke)
The First Dinosaurs. Burton / Dixon (Gareth Stevens)
Fossils Tell of Long Ago. Aliki (Harper & Row)
How to Draw Dinosaurs. LaPlaca (Troll)
Hunting the Dinosaurs and Other Prehistoric Animals. Burton / Dixon (Gareth Stevens)
The Last Dinosaurs. Burton / Dixon (Gareth Stevens)
Pteranodon. Wilson (Rourke)
Stegosaurus. Sheehan (Rourke)

New Words

Here are some new words from *The Jurassic Dinosaurs.* They appear for the first time in the text in *italics*, just as they appear here.

adapted .... changed to fit new needs

carcasses .... bodies of dead animals

carnivorous (car-NIV-er-us).. meat-eating

conifers (CON-if-ers) .... cone-bearing trees, usually evergreens

descended .... came down, or derived, from an earlier form

elongated .... grown in length

environment .... the natural home of any plant or animal

evolved .... developed by adapting and changing to suit changing environments

fossils .... the remains or traces of a plant or an animal. Fossils are preserved in sedimentary rock formations. Sedimentary rocks are rocks that are laid down in water.

gizzard .... a second stomach with thick, muscular walls and tough, horny lining for grinding food, usually with the addition of swallowed stones

impression .... a mark, imprint, or mold made by pressure

insulation .... protection from heat or cold

Jurassic .... one of the periods during which dinosaurs lived. It spanned 55 million years, from 135 to 190 million years ago.

membrane .... a thin sheet of skin or tissue

modified .... changed in form

paleontologist (pay-lee-on-TOL-o-gist)..... a scientist who studies fossils

piscivorous (pih-SIV-er-us) ... fish-eating

predators .... animals that kill other animals for food

scavenger .... an animal that eats the leftovers or carcasses of other animals

Index and Pronunciation Guide

Note: The use of a capital letter for an animal's name means that it is a specific *type*, or *genus*, of animal—like a Stegosaurus or Tyrannosaurus. The use of a lower case, or small, letter means that it is a member of a larger *group* of animals—like ichthyosaurs or crocodiles.